The DIABOLO from A to

"JUMBO"

"BIRDIE"

Family Diabolino

"ARLEQUINO"

"ARLEQUIN"

"CRISTAL"

Methodology :
Daniel Schambacher

Drawings :
Arnaud Toulon, Tours

Text :
Claude Camredon

Computer setting :
A Concept, Geneva

MISTER BABACHE
Jonglerie Diffusion S.A.

From the same publisher :

- « Diabolo Folies part 1 »
  (methodology for beginners - video VHS) (Geneva 1992)

- « Diabolo Folies part 2 »
  (advanced methodology - video VHS) (Geneva 1993)

- « La jonglerie, plaisir simple et facile »
  (in French) (Geneva 1994)

- instruction leaflets for beginners : « balls » (Geneva 1995)
  « clubs » (Geneva 1995)
  « devil sticks » (Geneva 1995)
  « scarves » (Geneva 1995)
  « diabolo » (Geneva 1995)

The Diabolo from A to Z Jonglerie Diffusion S.A. First edition July 1995

ISBN : 2-940065-10-1
Achévé d'imprimer en juillet 1995
Gibert Clarey Imprimeurs
N° 40868

TABLE OF CONTENTS - LISTING OF FIGURES

THE DIABOLO HISTORY

It is fairly difficult to know with precision when the diabolo was invented. Historians however agree that in China, where it was discovered, the game of diabolo has been practised for more than 4'000 years. It was named « Kouen-gen » during the Han dynasty (206 BC), which means « making the hollow bamboo whistle ». Indeed, in China today, diabolos are still made in bamboo, with openings on the side making it whistle while spinning. French and English missionaries and political envoys brought these strange objects back to Europe, named by an unknown erudite « DIABALLO » (later diabolo) from the Greek roots « dia » meaning across, and « ballo » meaning throw. In France, as soon as it was presented, the diabolo was well accepted and considered as a rival game to the « jeu de paume » probably the ancestor of tennis. As early as 1810, various clubs were formed in Paris and competitions held on what are today the Champs Elysées. The game of Diabolo became very fashionable and even the Court of Napoléon the First played with diabolo apparently made out of solid wood. In 1906, a French inventor Gustave Phillipart presented a diabolo made of 2 metal cups, with the edges protected by rubber cut from old tyres ! The modern diabolo was invented ! Soon a real craze for the diabolo started in France then in England. Numerous writings, stories and postcards show that diabolo was played everywhere by almost all social classes. With the First World War interest in the game declined. Later diabolo was only seen on stages in theatres. By 1980, thanks to the use of modern technology and materials, and research and precision in the manufacturing, a new era of the diabolo game started, allowing more and more jugglers and players to perform fantastic performances with 1, 2 or 3 of these strange and beautiful flying objects.

Diabolo, 4000 years of history, still a fabulous pastime with great potential for even more discoveries.

THE DIABOLO HISTORY (continued)

At the beginning of this century, the German artist McSouvereign held the unofficial title of « king of the diabolo » until 1947. Thereafter many artists took advantage of modern technology and the progress made in the manufacturing of better adapted diabolos and have transformed the game into a spectacular artform. Today, some « stars » of the diabolo have agreed to share their art with others and do not hesitate to explain their tricks and give advice. We would like to recognise and thank particularly :

- American Todd Strong, who had the vision, re-launched the game and trained thousands of jugglers.
- German Jochen Schell, called « Meister Schell » for his mastery of the Art with 2 and more diabolos.
- Frenchmen Thierry Nadalini for his elegance on top of his spectacular technique and
- Jean Manuel Thomas, most distinguished juggler with a remarquable imagination.
- Scot Donald Grant, who is breathtakingly shining on stage.
- the beautiful Maike Aerden, from Holland, who brilliantly represents the presence of women jugglers.
- Britons Guy Heathcote and Brendan Brolly, for their great and successful didactical energy.
- the young Swiss Laurent Perrelet who is opening the way to a new generation of jugglers.

Bibliography on the diabolo and its history :

J. Hembert et P. Nivoix, « Le Diabolo pour tous » (Imprimerie Duruy et Co, Paris 1908)
David Ward, « Diabolo, the game and its tricks » (Upcott Gill, London 1908)
D.W. Gould, « The Top » (Clarckson Potter Inc, New York 1973)
Todd Strong, « The Diabolo Book » (Brian Dubé Inc, New York 1994)
Todd Strong, « Diabolo Postcards » (Aragon Verlag, Moers 1994)
Jonglerie Diffusion, « Diabolo Folies » (VIDEO methodology in 2 parts, Jonglerie Diffusion, Geneva 1992)
Jonglerie Diffusion, « Le Diabolo de A à Z » french comics book (Jonglerie Diffusion, Geneva 1995)

Here is the object : its manufacturing is more intricate than it seems and the assembly requires much precision. The diabolo's balance must be perfect (each cup is marked), the structure rigid but shock-resistant (reinforced polyamid cones, rubber or Rextan cups). All materials must be of top quality to withstand abrasion and wear.

DIABOLO

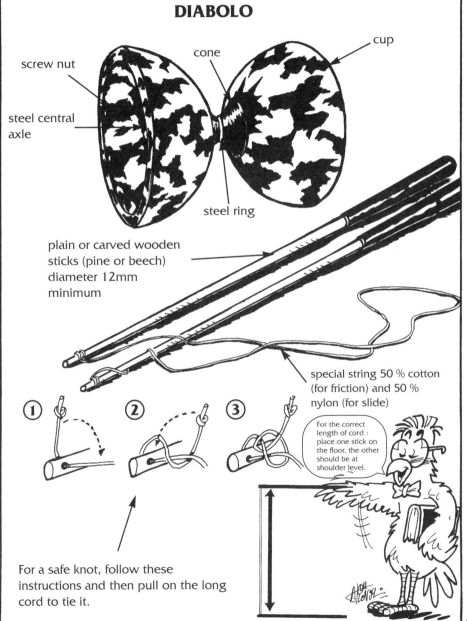

cup

cone

screw nut

steel central axle

steel ring

plain or carved wooden sticks (pine or beech) diameter 12mm minimum

special string 50 % cotton (for friction) and 50 % nylon (for slide)

① ② ③

For the correct length of cord : place one stick on the floor, the other should be at shoulder level.

For a safe knot, follow these instructions and then pull on the long cord to tie it.

POSITION

Terminology to better understand the instructions

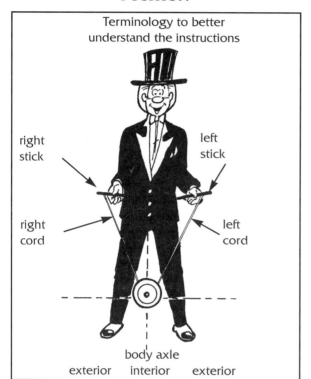

right stick

left stick

right cord

left cord

body axle

exterior   interior   exterior

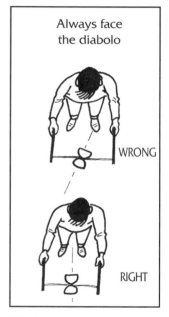

Always face the diabolo

WRONG

RIGHT

START UP

Place the diabolo to your right. Make it roll from right to left (right stick very low). When the diabolo is in front of you, on the body axle, lift it up with the right stick and accelerate the rotation with swift movements by the right wrist.

Attention : the diabolo rotates ALWAYS in the same direction

Generally, and always in this methodology, the acceleration is done by the right hand. Thanks in advance to all lefthanders for understanding that they must invert the instructions.

AXIS CORRECTIONS

An imperfect position of the body or of your arms or a spinning speed which is too slow will result in a loss of the desirable balance of the diabolo.

If the diabolo leans backwards (towards you) continue your accelerating movements with the right hand, but bring your right arm forward.

If the diabolo leans forwards (away from you) correct the inclination by accelerating with your right arm closer to your body (backwards from the original position).

CHANGE OF ORIENTATION

Should you wish to look at another section of the audience and show your better profile, here is the easy trick. Remember that you should always stay facing the diabolo.

To turn to the left (anti-clockwise) delicately touch the inside cup, close to you, with the tip of the right stick.

To turn to the right (clockwise) delicately touch the exterior cup with the tip of your right stick.

Attention : the shoulders should follow the rotating movement. Always stay facing the diabolo.

ACCELERATIONS

string in position 1	string in position 2	string in position 3

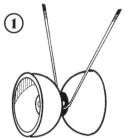  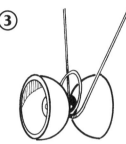

position 1 : diabolo on the string. The acceleration movement is soft and progressive and made by the right wrist. No bruque movements, no jumps, the string remains always in contact with the diabolo.

position 2 : twist the diabolo on the string 1 whole turn (360 degrees) The acceleration movements from the right hand are more powerful but remain supple. The acceleration will be faster because of the larger surface of friction on the diabolo ring. To unwind the string, do a sun.

position 3 : make a complete turn of string aroung the diabolo ring. Movements of the right wrist can be quite strong now, friction is very important and acceleration is immediate. Keep the strings stretched to prevent cramming around the ring. Recommended position for the Chinese acceleration (see next page).

CROSSING (fig. 1)

The favourite acceleration movement of Thierry Nadalini : the right arm gives the acceleration and passes alternatively over then under the left arm. Continue the movement to obtain high rotation speed.

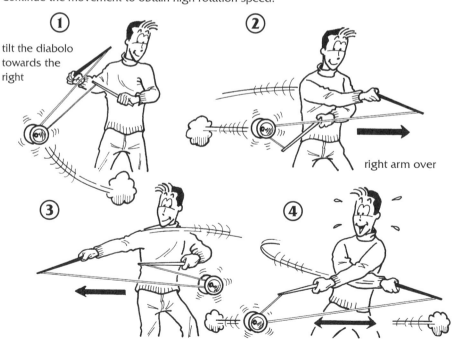

tilt the diabolo towards the right

right arm over

open towards the right

right arm under

JOCHEN SCHELL CHINESE ACCELERATION (fig. 2)

Place the strings in position 3 (see page 11) i.e. a complete turn around the diabolo axle.

Lower down the right hand.
The left arm keeps the string tight.

The right arm lifts the diabolo up rapidly.
The hand remains at head level.

The right arm then brings the diabolo downwards rapidly

By lifting and lowering the hand, with ample wrist movements, the diabolo gets a lot of spin. The left arm compensates for the brusque movements and keeps the string tight during the whole exercise.

Keep the string in position 3, of course,... or else beware of broken glass !

YOUR FIRST THROW (fig. 3)

① Give a lot of speed to your diabolo and align it properly (see page 10).

② Open your sticks to throw the diabolo.

③ Aim with the right stick, string at eye level and left hand pulling the string from below.

④ Catching is done close to the right stick.

⑤ The fall is broken with the right hand.

⑥ As soon as possible, accelerate the rotation with movements from the right hand and stabilize your diabolo.

SUNS

SUN TO THE BACK (fig. 4)

Both arms together and straight, start a big circle and follow the diabolo, sticks pointing up.

As the diabolo descends, bend the arms and point the sticks to the back. The diabolo will pass behind you to prevent any crossing of the strings.

Help the start of a new circle by rotating the shoulders. The diabolo is back in front.

PIROUETTE SUN (fig. 5)

Nice and easy figure to prevent the crossing of the strings. Keep arms and strings stretched, keep the diabolo in your sight. A pirouette from **left to right** slows down the rotation of the diabolo at the end of the figure, so accelerate as soon as possible. A pirouette from **right to left** allows you to throw the diabolo directly from the figure because of the acceleration given.

To keep the diabolo in control on the string, bring the tips of the sticks closer together.

SUNS TO THE SIDE (fig. 6)

Excellent training for controlling flight paths. Body position 1/4 turn to the left to face the side of the diabolo.

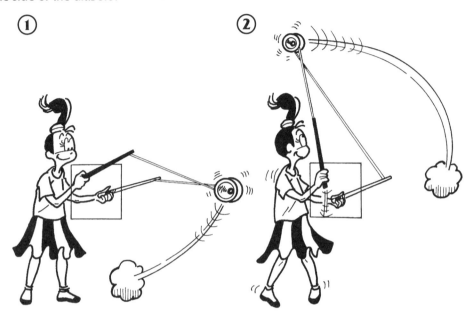

① Push the right stick forward to start the sun.

② Right stick follows the diabolo passing above the left shoulder.

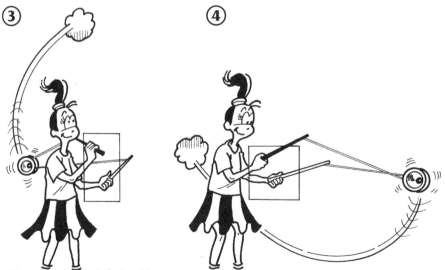

③ Right stick on the left shoulder. Left stick points outwards

④ Right stick restarts movement.

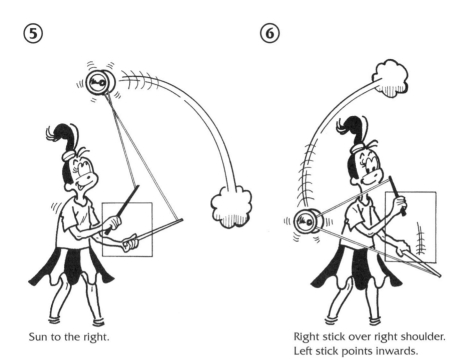

⑤ Sun to the right.

⑥ Right stick over right shoulder.
Left stick points inwards.

Right stick does all the restarting work and follow up.
Left stick follows the movement, keeps the strings tight and controls the stability of the diabolo.

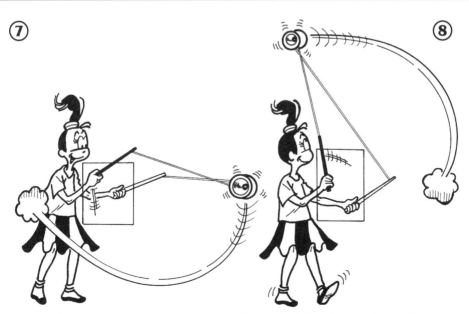

⑦ Right stick restarts movement.

⑧ Sun to the left again... and so on !

SUNS AND SCISSORS (fig. 7)

This nice figure is a good exercise for mastering the suns and preventing crossed strings.

Throw

To catch, cross the arms, right arm above.

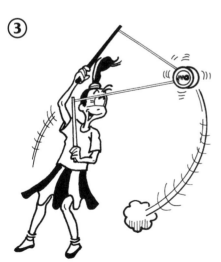

Push a sun to the right. The right stick pulls and goes first.

End of the sun, arms crossed, left arm above.

⑤

New sun towards the other side. If you go to the left, the left arm will go first and show the way.

⑥

End of the sun, arms crossed, right arm above.

⑦

To regain original position, push your arms outwards to free the diabolo and uncross your arms.

SUN FORWARD TO UNCROSS THE STRINGS (fig. 8)

Invented by Jean Manuel Thoma, this trick allows the uncrossing of the string and a more elegant posture during a series of figures.

As the diabolo goes up towards the left, place the right stick under the left one.

At the zenith, the right stick goes around the left one.

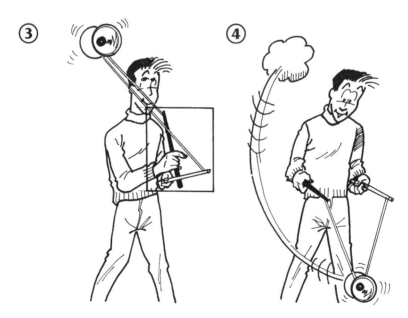

During the descent, the right stick is taken again by the right hand.

Ready for next figure !

SUN TO THE BACK AS AN EXIT (fig. 9)

① Throw

② Sticks pointing backwards, receive the diabolo at the back, to the right.

③ Sun towards the left. The movement starts by itself.

④ Keep the string tense. Give a slight traction, sticks together.

This figure, when made from right to left, gives a good spin to the diabolo.

SUN BETWEEN THE ARMS (fig. 10)

> Mind your nose, as the diabolo flies in front of you !

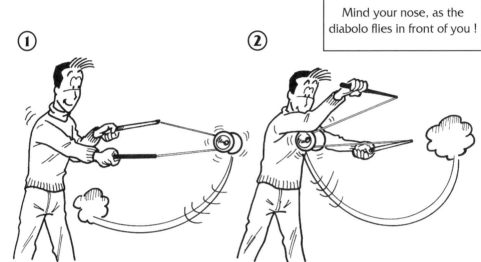

① Sticks pointed toward the inside, give some impulse to your diabolo by pushing it forward.

② As it comes back towards you, start the sun figure by pulling it up with the right hand. Left stick is pointed forward.

③ Right stick controls the diabolo and the spinning.

④ The acceleration is given by the right hand, as the diabolo starts its descent.

FIGURES AROUND YOU - USE YOUR BODY !

For all the following figures, a high spinning speed is recommended. Make sure that you control the acceleration methods explained in pages 12 and 13.

SATELLITE AROUND THE ARM (fig. 11)

Left stick at eye level and pointed towards the inside.
Right stick pointed backwards and towards the outside. String lightly touches your right arm.
Let the diabolo jump, by pulling on the left string.
Look to the right and receive the diabolo close to the right stick.
Carried by its own weight, the diabolo will pass under your arm.

SATELLITE AROUND BOTH ARMS (fig. 12)

Both sticks are pointed backwards and towards the outside. The string passes under both arms.
Let the diabolo jump by pulling the left stick.
Follow it visually.
Receive it close to the right stick.
The weight of the diabolo will make it pass under your arms without problem.

SATELLITE AROUND ONE LEG (fig. 13)

Place one leg above the string and let the diabolo slide to your left.
Pull on the left string to lift the diabolo.
Receive it close to the right stick to increase the spinning.
The diabolo, carried by its weight will pass easily.

BRIDGE OVER BOTH LEGS (fig. 14)

Part the sticks, pointing them towards the outside, pull the string and press it behind your legs. Absorb the fall of the diabolo on the string with a wrist movement and send it immediately to the other side. Keep a regular rhythm (throw - reception - throw) and ensure supple movements of your sticks.

23

SATELLITE WITH DOUBLE ORBIT (fig. 15)

Watch the spinning speed and the balance of the diabolo and ensure regular and smooth orbits. No brusque movements. To give more space to the diabolo, sway your hips a bit.

To have an orbit around your right leg, pass your left leg above the string and place your left hand in your back. Lift the diabolo by pulling it with the left hand. Receive it on the right string.

then

as the diabolo passes under your leg, point your right stick towards the left leg, bring back the left arm and throw the diabolo again. Continue the throws to the right and to the left.

TIE (fig. 16)

Hold both sticks firmly and pass the diabolo from one string to the other by short pushes with the sticks.

LITTLE BRIDGE (fig. 17)

Sticks are pointing backwards towards the outside. String is under the arms (see fig. 12, page 23) Hold your sticks firmly and move your arms in rhythm to absorb the falls and throw the diabolo again.

As soon as you control the passing of the diabolo under one leg, try to do it with one hand only !

Do fig. 13, page 23 and make sure that you have a lot of spin.

As the diabolo passes under your leg, quickly take both sticks in one hand, like scissors.

Exercise a gentle vertical movement to keep the diabolo going.

WHIP (fig. 19)

Throw vertically and open your arms.

Quickly, take both sticks, crossed, in your right hand. Place your index finger between the sticks and move a quarter of a turn to face the side of the diabolo.

Aim at the falling diabolo, and in a brisk movement whip it. The string will catch the diabolo.

KNEELING (fig. 20)

Exercise fig. 13 from page 23, then kneel down and keep a knee on the ground. Lift up the sticks to keep the string tight. Continue the same movement.
Do you want an additional impressive challenge?
From time to time, lift the diabolo higher and let it pass above your head!

SCARF (fig. 21)

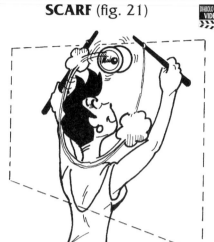

Arms lifted and head well tilted backwards, bring the string against your neck. Point your sticks backwards, your arms well separated to leave space for the diabolo. Keep your head still, but follow the diabolo with your eyes. The diabolo remains within a vertical plan, behind your head. The figure is quite impressive but not that difficult. Don't worry about your ears, the weight of the diabolo will make it pass away from them!

TOREADOR (fig. 22)

The left stick goes behind you and the diabolo to your right. With both hands, lift it above your head.

Bring the right arm behind you and receive the diabolo on your left. Then throw again to your right and take the first position (left arm behind you) to receive the diabolo on your right.

SCISSORS UNDER THE LEG (fig. 23)

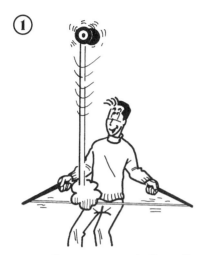

(1) Open your arms to throw the diabolo.

(2) Bring the left stick in front of you and receive the diabolo with crossed arms.

(3) Bring the diabolo down and pass the right stick under your right leg.

(4) Pull simultaneously on both sticks and the diabolo will be thrown between your legs.

(5) Uncross and receive the diabolo in normal position.

TWIST (fig. 24)

String behind you, let the diabolo
come to your right, under your
arm. Then throw it in front of
you. Follow the flight path.

Quickly, bring your left arm
behind you and the right arm in
front of you to your left. Make a
quarter turn with your shoulders.
Keep the string tight.

Practise the figure first
without diabolo, to
speed up the precise
movement of the
string.

If you follow the diabolo flight
well the catch is really
spectacular !
You can do the same on the
other side, of course.

CHINESE PIROUETTE EXPRESS (fig. 24)

The key to success for this number is the position and pivoting of the feet. First, without the diabolo, try to turn very rapidly on the spot.

Place your left foot in front of the right one. Your diabolo remains very close to the right stick.

Pivot around your right foot.

Lift up the diabolo, at first approximately 30 cm, (later, much less).

Start with legs crossed. Place your diabolo well to your right.

Keep arms straight and string tight.

Receive the diabolo in motion while turning, right stick in a low position.

To stop the pirouette, rest your left foot.

SCISSORS TO THE BACK (fig. 25)

① Lift the diabolo and rapidly bring the right stick to the left.

② Catch the diabolo by passing the string over it.

③ Right arm at your back, let the diabolo slide to your left.

The same figure can be made from left to right but will require a faster spinning of the diabolo (initial movement slows down the rotation).

④ Then open both sticks to throw the diabolo over your shoulder.

SUN AROUND THE ARMS (fig. 26)

① With the diabolo on your left, pass the right string over your right forearm and lift the diabolo about 20 cm. only.

② Catch from above with the left string.

③ Start a sun by bringing the left arm under the right arm. The string will cross.

④ Keep the arms in position, string will uncross by itself. Re- activate the movement.

TRICKS WITH HANDSTICKS

POSITION OF THE STICKS (fig. 27)

When your diabolo hits a stick, it will tend to gather momentum and roll.
To keep control, tilt your stick. Direction will depend on the rotation and in which hand is the stick.

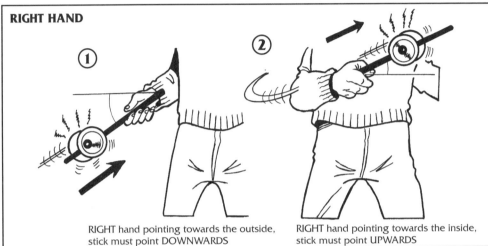

RIGHT HAND

① RIGHT hand pointing towards the outside, stick must point DOWNWARDS

② RIGHT hand pointing towards the inside, stick must point UPWARDS

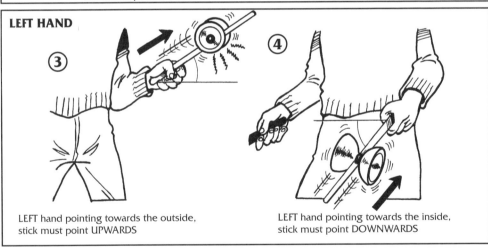

LEFT HAND

③ LEFT hand pointing towards the outside, stick must point UPWARDS

④ LEFT hand pointing towards the inside, stick must point DOWNWARDS

Be careful ! your diabolo always spins from right to left !
Think of the position of the stick, or else.....

ZOU!!!

BALANCE OF THE DIABOLO (fig. 28)

For all tricks with sticks, the diabolo must remain perfectly balanced.

If the LEFT cup is too low,

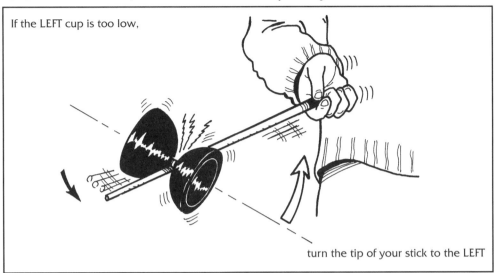

turn the tip of your stick to the LEFT

If the RIGHT cup is too low,

turn the tip of your stick to the RIGHT

This movement is also useful to correct the balance while juggling with 2 diabolos. One diabolo continues to spin on the string while the other's balance is corrected on the stick.

TRICKS WITH STICKS

FIRST TRIALS (fig. 29)

Let a diabolo roll from the string onto the stick.

Bring it back on the string and accelerate the spin.

Then roll it onto the other stick. Repeat this exercise a few times.

THROWS (fig. 30)

Right stick pointing to the inside, lift the diabolo onto it.

Same exercise with the left stick pointing to the inside.

Make the flight longer by pointing the right stick to the outside.

Do the same with the left stick pointing also to the outside.

Think of the inclination of the sticks to keep control of the diabolo (see fig. 27, page 32).

TIT FOR TAT (fig. 31)

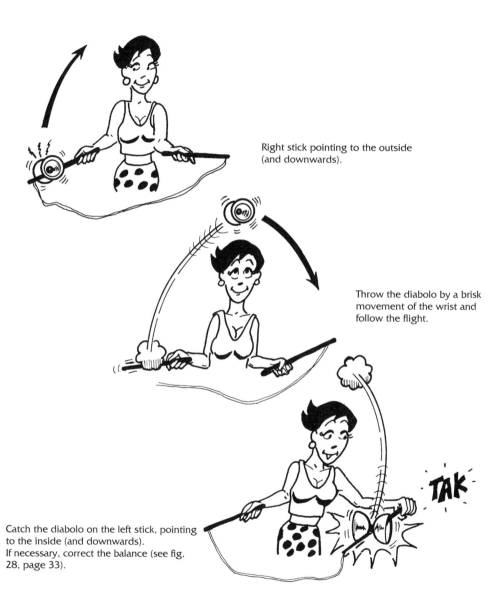

Right stick pointing to the outside (and downwards).

Throw the diabolo by a brisk movement of the wrist and follow the flight.

Catch the diabolo on the left stick, pointing to the inside (and downwards).
If necessary, correct the balance (see fig. 28, page 33).

TAK

MATADOR (fig. 32)

Throw the diabolo onto the left stick, pointing downwards.

Slowly bring the stick and diabolo behind you, then under your right arm, maintaining the inclination.

With a movement of the wrist, throw the diabolo in front of your right arm.

Then give immediately some additional spin.

CARPET BEATER (fig. 33)

The diabolo is on the right stick, pointing to the outside and downwards.
With a vertical movement of the wrist, throw the diabolo above your right shoulder.

Catch it falling on the other side of the same stick, pointing upwards. Throw again.

TAK

Be careful when throwing : use a supple vertical movement, or else the diabolo dissappears !

TAK

Receive it on the right stick, pointing downwards.

FLAMENCO (fig. 34)

From the right stick, throw the diabolo and follow its flight carefully.

Catch it with the left stick under the leg. Olé !

SCISSORS TO END A FIGURE (fig. 35)

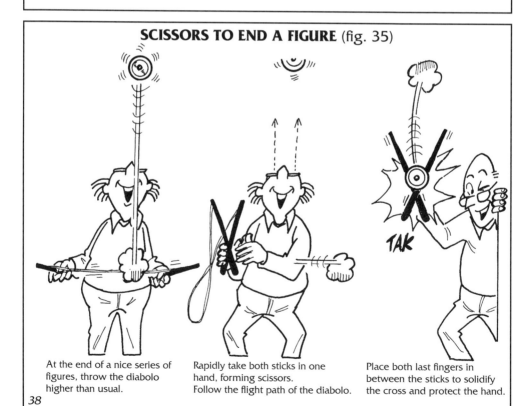

At the end of a nice series of figures, throw the diabolo higher than usual.

Rapidly take both sticks in one hand, forming scissors.
Follow the flight path of the diabolo.

Place both last fingers in between the sticks to solidify the cross and protect the hand.

GAMES AND CHALLENGES

LIFT WITH ONE HAND (fig. 36)

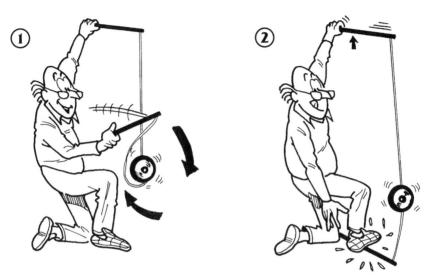

With the string of the right stick, turn around the diabolo axis once, from the front and toward the outside. Your left hand is placed above your head. Your foot holds the right stick on the ground. Place the left stick vertically above. A light gentle pull of the left hand will bring up your diabolo, like a lift.

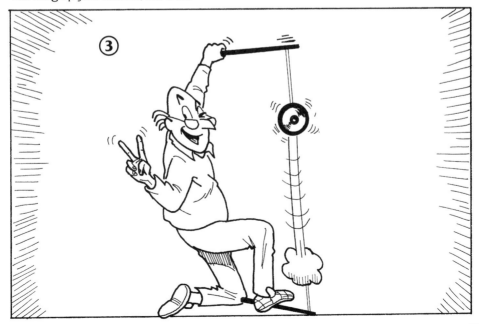

TIGHTROPE WALKER (fig. 37)

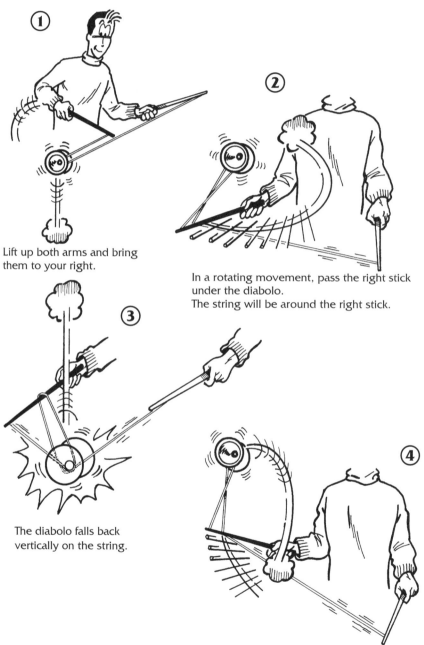

①

Lift up both arms and bring them to your right.

②

In a rotating movement, pass the right stick under the diabolo.
The string will be around the right stick.

③

The diabolo falls back vertically on the string.

④

To free the diabolo, push the right stick to the outside and upwards.
The diabolo will come back in place automatically.

TIGHTROPE WALKER IN A LIFT (fig. 38)

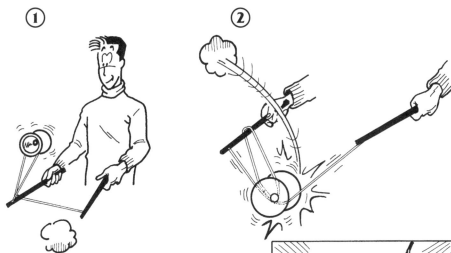

Make a tightrope walker figure (see fig. 37, page 40).

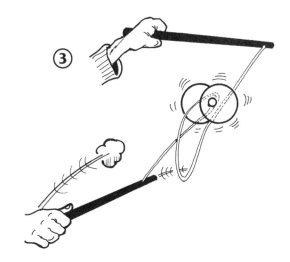

Lift up the diabolo vertically at chest level and take away the right stick. Gently pull the string tight.

At each traction downwards, the diabolo will take the lift !

These figures slow down the diabolo spin a lot. Do not forget to accelerate the spin after each exercice.

DIABOLO ON RING (fig. 39)

①

Hold your ring firmly and pass it under the diabolo.

②

Lift it up and take the diabolo off the string.

Watch the rotation speed !

AXIS CORRECTION WITH A RING (fig. 40)

If the right cup is too low, turn the ring towards the right, on its vertical axle.

Turn the ring towards the left and you will lift up the left side of the diabolo.

WALK IN THE RING (fig. 41)

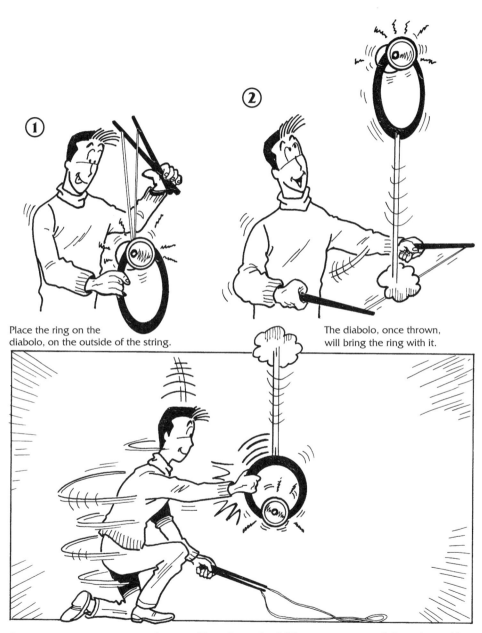

① Place the ring on the diabolo, on the outside of the string.

② The diabolo, once thrown, will bring the ring with it.

Do a quarter turn to receive the ring. Slow down the fall by a movement of the wrist and by bending your legs slightly to keep the balance of the diabolo.

Check the rotation speed prior to the throw.

Go towards the diabolo.

To ensure the landing, tilt the ring. Then place the ring vertical to slow down the fall and prevent braking the diabolo's spin.

Tilt the ring again for the next throw.

Receive the diabolo on the string. Accelerate the rotation.

SKIPPING ROPE (fig. 43)

First, skip without the diabolo and look upwards. Then, throw the diabolo at least 3 meters high. Later you will throw less high or else do a double skip. Skip with your knees well up and keep the elbows close to your body to allow the string to pass rapidly over your head.

FLEA (fig. 44)

The string remains between your eyes and the diabolo, on a vertical plane.
For the exercise use short movements of the arms and shoulders.
Keep the arms well apart. The figure should be done from right to left.

ROLLING DUO (fig. 45)

DIABOLO FOLIES
VIDEO

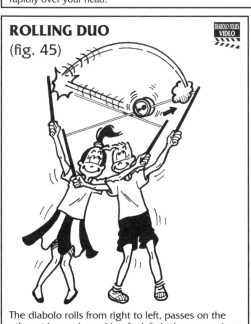

The diabolo rolls from right to left, passes on the other string and, reaching far left, is thrown again to the right stick of the partner. Both strings are crossed in the same vertical plane.

SATELLITE ON ONE FOOT (fig. 46)

DIABOLO FOLIES
VIDEO

Place your right foot on the string. Left hand will make the diabolo jump. The weight of the diabolo will make it pass under the foot. (see fig. 13, page 23)

UMBRELLA (fig. 47)

 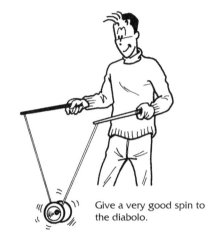

Give a very good spin to
the diabolo.

The right hand starts a sun
towards the right side.

When the diabolo is on top, the right
stick points towards the left.

④

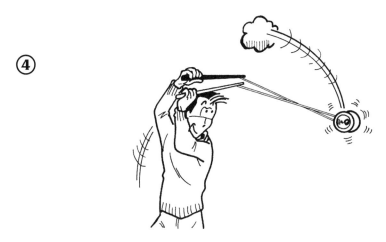

Lift both arms, right arm above, sticks horizontal to keep the diabolo at shoulder level.

⑤

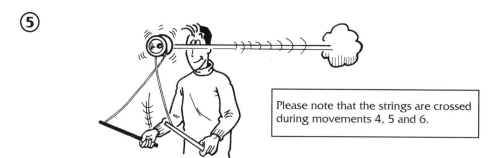

Please note that the strings are crossed during movements 4, 5 and 6.

Then pull on the strings and bring both arms down in one simultaneous movement.
The diabolo flies in front of you quite rapidly.

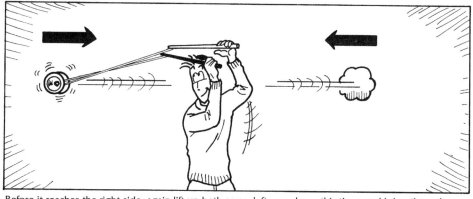

Before it reaches the right side, again lift up both arms, left arm above this time, and bring them down to send the diabolo to the left.
Continue the umbrella figure by repeating movements 4 - 5 - 6 - 4 - 5 - 6 - etc.

LOOK... NO STICKS !

TIGHTROPE WALKER WITH A FLYING STICK (fig. 48)

①

Start a tightrope walker figure (see fig. 37, page 40)

②

Lift your left hand up to shoulder level.

③

Let the left stick go. It will be taken along by the weight of the diabolo.

④

Bring your open hand forward above your right stick to catch the flying stick.

LETTING GO DURING A SUN (fig. 49)

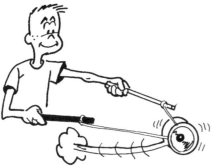

Swing your diabolo and then start a sun towards your left side.

At the peak of the sun (12 o'clock) let the right stick go.

Attention : 12 o'clock is the time to let it go !

Follow the flight of the stick.

PAF

Bring your open hand forward to meet the stick (see fig. 48, page 48).

BIG DIPPER (fig. 50)

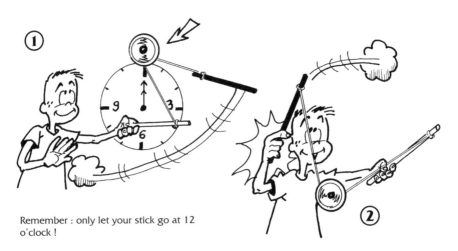

Remember : only let your stick go at 12 o'clock !

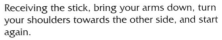

The flight path of the diabolo looks like an infinity sign. (figure 8 lying down)

Receiving the stick, bring your arms down, turn your shoulders towards the other side, and start again.

Launch a sun to the other side. At 12 o'clock, let the stick go.

Do not try to grab the flying stick, just go with your open hand towards it.

LET IT GO UNDER THE LEG (fig. 51)

Launch a sun from left to right and place a leg over the string.
(see fig. 13, page 23)

Follow the stick as far as possible under the leg and let it go when the diabolo is at 12 o'clock.

To receive the stick, extend your hand to meet it.

LET IT GO IN THE LIFT (fig. 52)

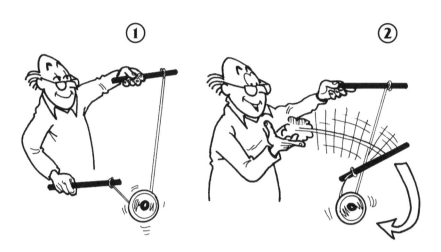

① Give a lot of spin to your diabolo. Place yourself to the side of the diabolo and lift up your left hand.

② Throw the right stick in front on you.

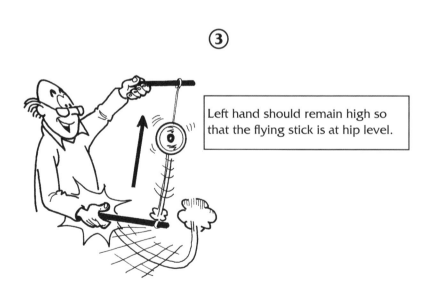

③

Left hand should remain high so that the flying stick is at hip level.

Receive the stick, pull delicately downwards and your diabolo will take the lift !

LET IT GO BEHIND THE BACK (fig. 53)

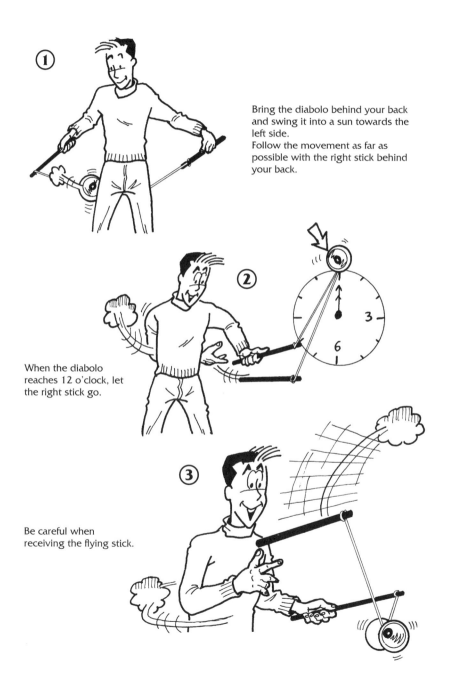

① Bring the diabolo behind your back and swing it into a sun towards the left side.
Follow the movement as far as possible with the right stick behind your back.

② When the diabolo reaches 12 o'clock, let the right stick go.

③ Be careful when receiving the flying stick.

ABANDON BOTH STICKS (fig. 54)

Launch a sun towards the right side, with both arms stretched. When the diabolo reaches 12 o'clock, let both sticks go at the same time.

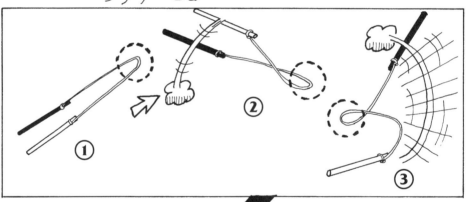

During the rotation, the left stick (white) will have more impetus and will catch up then overtake the right stick.
Catch the first arriving stick, the left one, with your right hand. Be careful, the sticks will cross and arrive very fast.

Remember : change of sticks = crossed string. Elementary, my dear !

FAN (fig. 55)

①

Both sticks in one hand, take the left string with your forefinger.

②

Throw the diabolo vertically by pushing up with both arms.

③ Receive the diabolo on the double string.

④ Use the momentum of the falling diabolo to launch a sun towards the right side, still holding the string. At the peak of the diabolo trajectory, let both sticks go at the same time.

⑤ PAF

Hand wide open to meet the flying sticks.

KNITTING

SWISS CUCKOO CLOCK (fig. 56)

Right hand passes above the left stick.

And pulls down, half way between the stick and the diabolo.

Push on the strings and swing the left hand backwards.

cuckoo ! cuckoo !

STEAM ENGINE (fig. 57)

① Take the left string in your hand.

② Left stick horizontal, pass the right string above it so that the string forms a triangle.

③ Slide the right stick (black) inside the triangle as far as possible.

Important : push the stick forward to at least 2/3 of its length so that the segment AB does not hinder the movements of the diabolo.

Do a satellite around the right stick, by rotating clockwise.

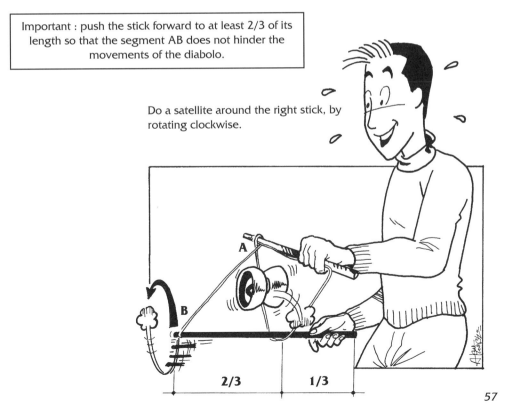

A

B

2/3   1/3

CROSS (fig. 58)

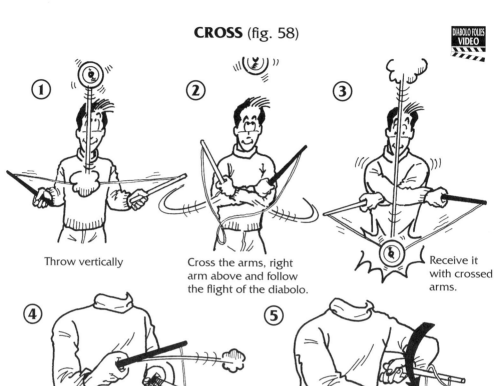

① Throw vertically

② Cross the arms, right arm above and follow the flight of the diabolo.

③ Receive it with crossed arms.

④ Uncross the arms by letting the right string pass over the left stick.

⑤ With right stick take the left string from underneath.

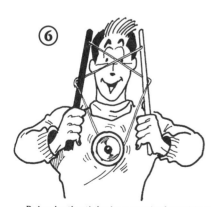

⑥ Raise both sticks in a vertical position.

⑦ Throw the diabolo onto the cross. Tilt both sticks forward to avoid the strings.

CROSS EXPRESS (fig. 59)

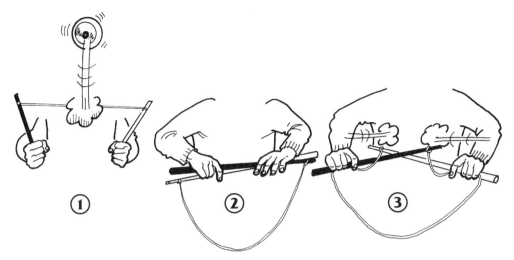

① Throw carefully : rather high and vertically.

② Swing the sticks one against the other, in a horizontal position.

③ Rapidly spread your arms, keeping your fingers clutched. The string will remain in your hands.

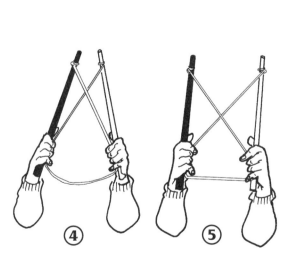

④ Set both sticks upright, keeping the string between your fingers.

⑤ Hold the string firmly and receive the diabolo on this cross.

DOUBLE CROSS (fig. 60)

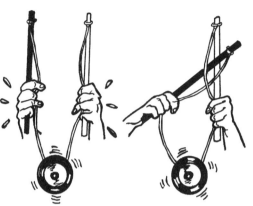

Raise the sticks vertically and grasp the strings.

Bring the right stick between the left one and its string.

Spread the sticks, then pass the left stick between the right one and its string.

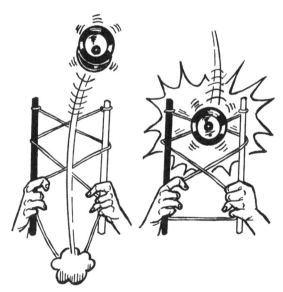

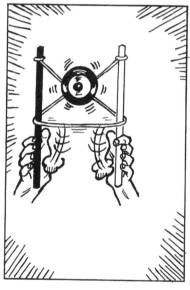

Spread the sticks again to form the « double cross » and throw the diabolo.

Hold the string firmly for the reception of the diabolo.

Open your fingers and the « double cross » turns into a « simple cross ».

MAGIC KNOT (fig. 61)

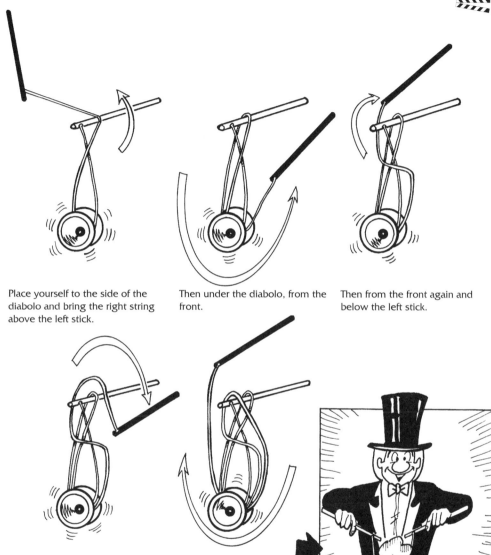

Place yourself to the side of the diabolo and bring the right string above the left stick.

Then under the diabolo, from the front.

Then from the front again and below the left stick.

Finally, above the left stick.

Then turn around the diabolo

Tilt both sticks forward and the diabolo will free itself.

DIABOLO PLAY WITH A PARTNER

ROLLING PASS
(fig. 62)

The diabolo rolls on the string from right to left (if you are right handed). Let it roll gently on the horizontal tight string between the partners.
The return comes from above !

CROSSED PASSES
(fig. 63)

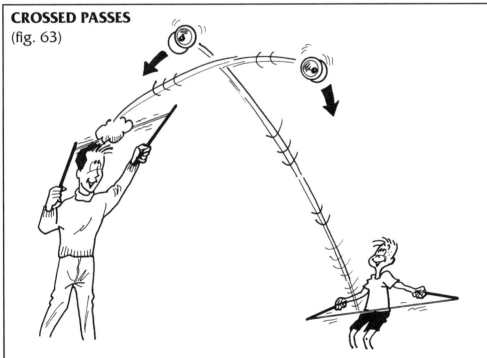

Throw by a supple wrist movement to ensure a safe flight.
Receive the diabolo close to the right stick to get some more spin.

ACROBATIC PASSES (fig. 64)

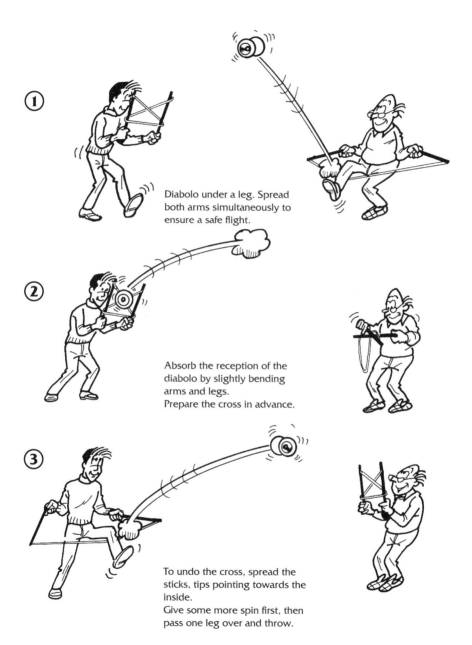

(1) Diabolo under a leg. Spread both arms simultaneously to ensure a safe flight.

(2) Absorb the reception of the diabolo by slightly bending arms and legs.
Prepare the cross in advance.

(3) To undo the cross, spread the sticks, tips pointing towards the inside.
Give some more spin first, then pass one leg over and throw.

PASSING... WITHOUT STICKS (fig. 65)

①

Give a lot of spin and then do a tightrope walker (see fig. 37, page 40).

②

③

Lift the left hand and let the stick go.
Arlequin does 1/4 turn to the right to face the arrival of the flying stick.

Arm stretched, hand open in front to grasp the stick as early as possible.

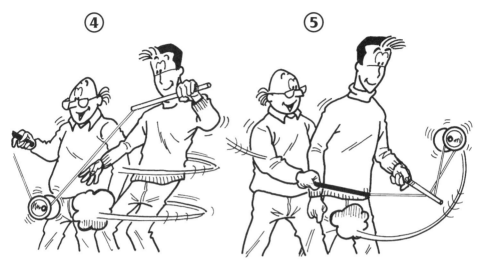

④ Jumbo and Arlequin take the
original position, side by side.

⑤ Then tightrope walker to the left side. Jumbo follows
the stick with a shoulders movement. Arlequin
passes his stick under the diabolo.

⑥ Jumbo lifts his right hand,
then lets the stick go.

PAF

Arm stretched, hand open in front Arlequin grasps
the stick as early as possible.

FAN IN DUO (fig. 66)

① Do a fan (see fig. 55, page 55).

② Go towards arriving sticks.

③ Both partners lower their arms.

④ Then simultaneously tighten the string.

⑤ Receive the diabolo and give more spin.

SATELLITE AROUND YOUR PARTNER (fig. 67)

①

Pass the first arm when the diabolo is in the air, then do a « satellite around one arm ».

②

Then pass the other arm to do a « satellite around both arms ».

③

Spread the sticks according to your partner's tummy !

SATELLITE AROUND YOUR PARTNER'S ARMS (fig. 68)

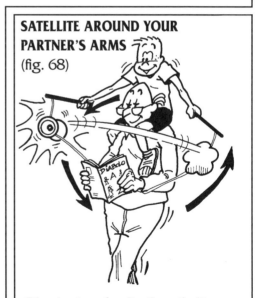

Take advantage of reading the method to give good advice !

TABLE TENNIS (fig. 69)

Arlequino throws the diabolo vertically and receives the second one.

Birdie does the pass.

Arlequino tilts the string to ensure a safer throw to Birdie.

Don't forget the spin !

PASSES WITH 3 DIABOLOS - with assistant (fig. 70)

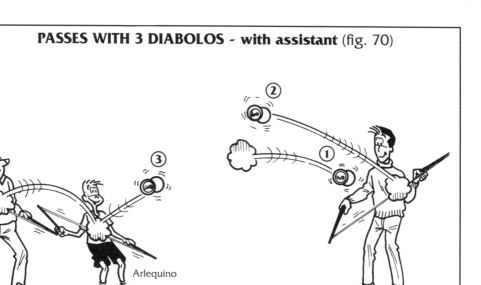

Arlequino throws diabolo 1 to Arlequin.
Arlequin throws diabolo 2 to Arlequino and at the same time.
Jumbo throws diabolo 3 to Arlequino.
Arlequino throws diabolo 3 to Arlequin
then both jugglers exchange diabolos. As soon as a diabolo is received, it is
immediately thrown back.

PASSES WITH 3 DIABOLOS - no assistant (fig. 71)

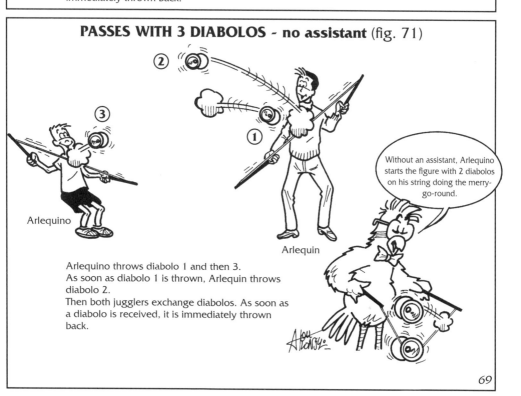

Arlequino throws diabolo 1 and then 3.
As soon as diabolo 1 is thrown, Arlequin throws
diabolo 2.
Then both jugglers exchange diabolos. As soon as
a diabolo is received, it is immediately thrown
back.

PASSES WITHIN THE FAMILY (fig. 72)

①

Each juggler passes to the immediate partner, from left to right to help the spin of the diabolo.
The last one throws above all others to the first juggler.....

②

..... if all agree !

JUGGLING WITH 2 DIABOLOS

RECOMMENDATIONS

With 2 diabolos, the RIGHT STICK accelerates, commands, corrects the axis of both diabolos.
For better control of the diabolos, the sticks point towards the interior.
The left hand lifts the diabolos and passes them on to the right string.

MERRY-GO-ROUND WITH ASSISTANT (fig. 74)

Arlequino places the white diabolo firmly on the string. This will make the black diabolo jump onto the right string. Arlequino keeps hold of the white diabolo and follows the trajectory of the black one.

MERRY-GO-ROUND SOLO (fig. 75)

Arlequin is waiting, with arms spread and diabolo 2 in rotation on the string.
Arlequino throws diabolo 1 to the right of the juggler.

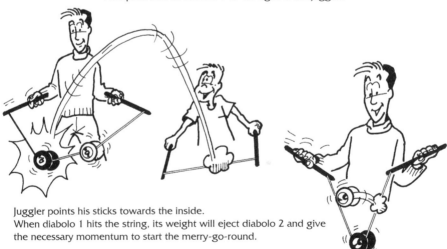

Juggler points his sticks towards the inside.
When diabolo 1 hits the string, its weight will eject diabolo 2 and give the necessary momentum to start the merry-go-round.

To keep the rotation going, the right stick is lowered and lifted in a vertically elliptical movement. (see the movement of the satellite fig. 11, page 23).

AXIS CORRECTIONS

Still keeping the merry-go-round in action, with the right stick gently touch one of the diabolo cups.

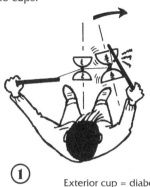

① Exterior cup = diabolo will turn towards the right.

② Interior cup = diabolo will turn towards the left.

CORRECTION OF BALANCE

Still keeping the merry-go-round in action, the right stick is gently placed sideways on both cups.

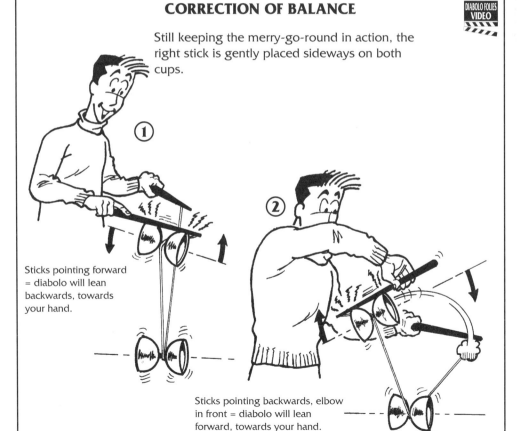

① Sticks pointing forward = diabolo will lean backwards, towards your hand.

② Sticks pointing backwards, elbow in front = diabolo will lean forward, towards your hand.

GRIPS AND THROWS

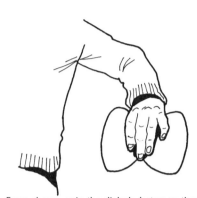

From above : grip the diabolo between thumb and middle finger. The other fingers hold the balance.

Throw with a wrist movement upwards, lifting the forearm.
This throw can be done by both hands, but always from the right side.

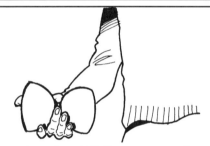

From underneath : middle finger presses on the diabolo ring, the other fingers lead the movement.

Throw while pulling the hand backwards, bending the wrist towards yourself, and flexing the forearm. Throw in front of you with the right hand.

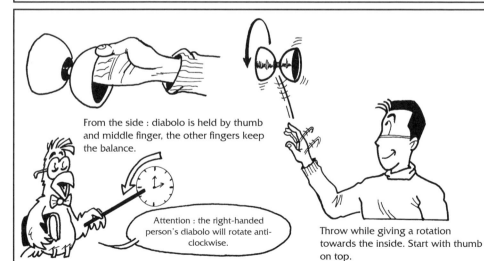

From the side : diabolo is held by thumb and middle finger, the other fingers keep the balance.

Attention : the right-handed person's diabolo will rotate anti-clockwise.

Throw while giving a rotation towards the inside. Start with thumb on top.

MERRY - GO - ROUND WITHOUT ASSISTANT (fig. 76)

Hold both sticks in one hand in a « V » position.
Ensure that the diabolo has a lot of spin.
Throw the second diabolo. The way to throw is
your choice.

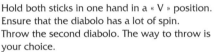

Rapidly grasp the sticks.

The reception of the falling diabolo on the right
side of the string will start the merry-go-round.
Do not forget to point both sticks towards the
inside as soon as possible.

MERRY-GO-ROUND YO-YO (fig. 77)

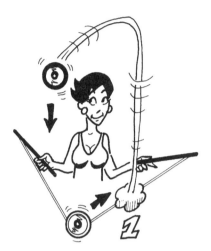

During the merry-go-round, throw a diabolo at head level by pulling from the left hand. The other diabolo remains on the string.

At reception of the falling diabolo, its weight will again start the merry-go-round.

During the throws, do not forget to increase periodically the spin of both diabolos, for example by starting merry-go-rounds again. You should also correct axis and balance (see page 73).

BIG MERRY-GO-ROUND (fig. 78)

As explained in fig. 77 (above) this time throw the diabolo well above your head. The merry-go-round gets much bigger.

COLUMNS (fig. 79)

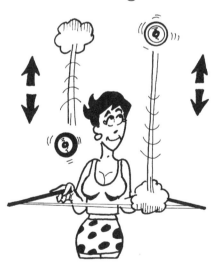

Instead of throwing as in the previous figure, throw each diabolo vertically, in columns.

MERRY-GO-ROUND ON THE RIGHT STICK (fig. 80)

A small throw from the left side will pass the diabolo onto the right stick.

Free the diabolo by inclining the stick downwards and start the merry-go-round again.

Remember the sticks' inclinations to control the diabolo (see fig. 27, page 32).

MERRY-GO-ROUND ON THE LEFT STICK (fig. 81)

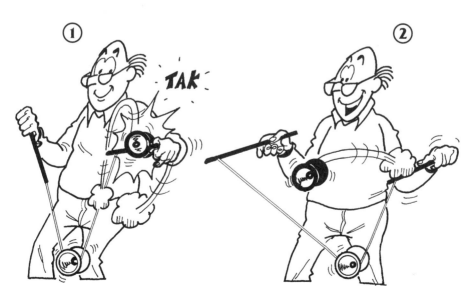

A small vertical throw from the left side will bring the diabolo onto the left stick.

Then throw the diabolo from the left stick onto the right string and start the merry-go-round again.

77

MERRY-GO-ROUND SATELLITE AROUND ONE ARM (fig. 82)

 ①

 ②

During a merry-go-round figure, point the right stick backwards and rapidly bring the string under the arm.

The left stick gives the necessary impulse to lift the diabolo above the shoulder.

The left hand throws the diabolo, the right hand accelerates the spin and corrects the axis.

MERRY-GO-ROUND SATELLITE AROUND ONE LEG (fig. 83)

 ①

 ②

As soon as the black diabolo touches the string on the right side, pass the leg over the string.

The white diabolo will pass above the leg.

JUMPING MERRY-GO-ROUND (fig. 84)

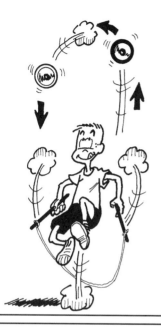

Make a big merry-go-round (see fig. 78, page 76) then skip (see fig. 43, page 45).
Throw the diabolos at least 2.5 meters above your head.

ENDING WITH CROSSED STICKS (fig. 85)

① During the merry-go-round, throw a diabolo vertically, the other one stays on the string.
Take both sticks in one hand.

② Follow the recommendations of fig. 35, page 38, to protect your hand and fingers.

TAK

ROCKET START UP (fig. 86)

Black diabolo on the string, on the floor in front of you, near your right foot.

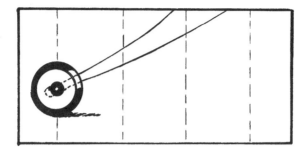

Place white diabolo on both strings, to the right of the black diabolo.

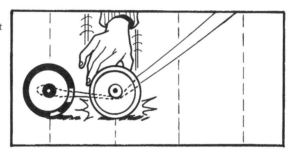

Take the black diabolo and pass it over the white one, to rest on the other side, on both strings.

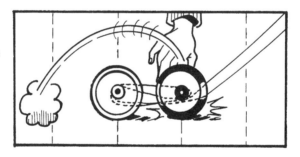

Do the same with the white diabolo.

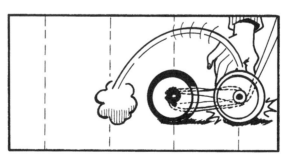

Important : for clarity, the diabolos on the drawings are placed as seen by the juggler and well spaced. In reality, make sure that the diabolos touch each other to enable them to lean on each other during take off.

ROCKET START UP - BLAST OFF ! (still fig. 86)

①

Both diabolos are on your right.

②

Pull the sticks upwards, in a big vertical move. The white diabolo will be propelled above your head, slightly to your left.

③

Rapidly grasp both sticks.

④

Receive the white diabolo on the right of your string. Its fall will start a merry-go-round.

MERRY-GO-ROUND WITH REBOUND (fig. 87)

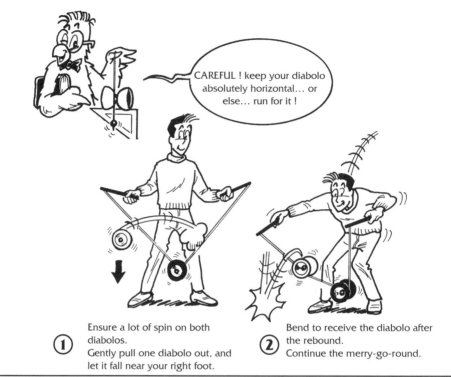

CAREFUL ! keep your diabolo absolutely horizontal… or else… run for it !

(1) Ensure a lot of spin on both diabolos.
Gently pull one diabolo out, and let it fall near your right foot.

(2) Bend to receive the diabolo after the rebound.
Continue the merry-go-round.

YOKE (fig. 88)

During the merry-go-round, lift up your right foot.

When the black diabolo arrives on the left string, lower both sticks and lift the foot higher against the string. This will stop the merry-go-round and the string will form a W sign on which the diabolos continue to spin. By throwing the white diabolo with the left stick onto the right string and by removing your foot, you will start the merry-go-round again.

MERRY-GO-ROUND WITH PIROUETTE (fig. 89)

As soon as the white diabolo touches the right string, start the lift by rotating the shoulders towards the left side.

When the left stick is at shoulder level and the black diabolo passes above the white one, do a pirouette with stretched arms (see fig. 5, page 15).

Keep the arms stretched until the end of the pirouette to make space for the diabolos.

Start the merry-go-round again with the white diabolo.

INFERNAL CHASE (fig. 88)

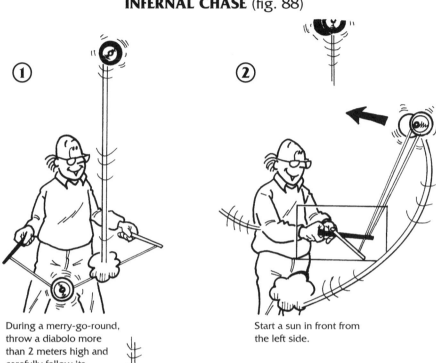

(1) During a merry-go-round, throw a diabolo more than 2 meters high and carefully follow its trajectory.

(2) Start a sun in front from the left side.

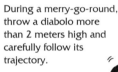

(3) Exchange the sticks to uncross the string (see fig. 8, page 20).

(4) Receive the black diabolo and it will restart the merry-go-round.

Focus on the flying diabolo.
To train for this figure, take one diabolo and try the sun in front while looking up all the time.

MERRY-GO-ROUND WITHOUT STICKS (fig. 89)

When the white diabolo touches the string at the right, start swinging both sticks towards the left as in fig. 49, page 49.

When the black diabolo is at its peak (12 o'clock), let the right stick go.

With open hand, move towards the flying stick.

A flying stick can have an unexpected trajectory !
After reception, ensure that both strings remain in a parallel plane to the juggler.
The merry-go-round has started again, all alone, thanks to the black diabolo.

CATCHING ON THE CROSS (fig. 90)

During a merry-go-round, throw the black diabolo, while the white one remains on the string.
Pass the left string onto the right stick.

Notice that the string is crossed above the white diabolo.
Then, bring the left stick under the right one.

Set both sticks upright to form a new cross.

Hold sticks firmly to receive the black diabolo.

To get back to the original figure (merry-go-round) throw the black diabolo again, undo the cross by tilting both sticks forwards. Receive the black diabolo on the right string and the merry-go-round will launch itself again.

DIABOLO TENNIS

Surface : a volley ball or badminton court or the service squares of a tennis court.

Objectives : Maintain the diabolo in the air as long as possible by throwing it above a net to a receiving team. Try to make them lose control of the diabolo.

Rules :
- 1 team serves (makes the first throw) during 5 points. First team reaching 15 points wins. Change side after each game.
- diabolo must be kept spinning by the serving team otherwise the point does not count.
- diabolo cannot touch the ground or this will give 1 point to the other team.
- diabolo must remain within the field limit (otherwise 1 point to the other team).
- net cannot be touched by players or diabolo (otherwise 1 point to the other team).
- players can move around the field as they like.
For safety reasons, use only rubber diabolos !
Game can be played by 1 or more players on each side.

JUGGLING WITH THREE DIABOLOS

START UP WITH ONE SPINNING DIABOLO (fig. 91)

(1)

Diabolo 3 on the string has a lot of spin. Diabolo 2 is in the left hand. Both handsticks are crossed in one hand, ready to be very quickly taken.

To start, hold diabolo 1 and 2 parallel to diabolo 3 already on the string.

(2)

With the right hand throw diabolo 1 more than 3 meters high.

(3)

Rapidly take diabolo 2 in the right hand.

(4)

Throw diabolo 2 also 3 meters high, then grasp both handsticks.

Spread the sticks wide to throw diabolo 3
vertically.

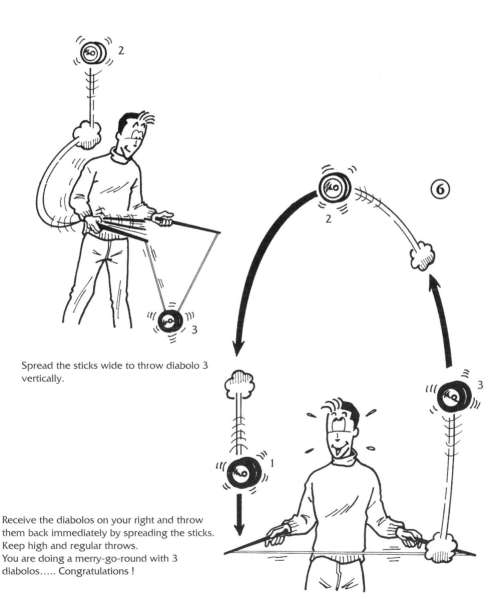

Receive the diabolos on your right and throw
them back immediately by spreading the sticks.
Keep high and regular throws.
You are doing a merry-go-round with 3
diabolos..... Congratulations !

START UP WITH TWO SPINNING DIABOLOS (fig. 92)

Make a merry-go-round then take both sticks, well spread, in your left hand.

Throw diabolo 3 with the right hand.

Then grasp the handsticks, and throw successively diabolos 1 and 2 more than 3 meters high.
Continue as explained in figure 91, page 89.

START UP WITH TWO DIABOLOS - WITH ASSISTANCE (fig. 93)

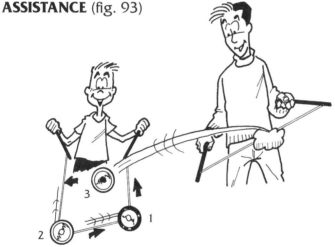

Arlequin spins diabolo 3 and as soon as diabolo 2 is in the air, throws it between the strings.

Arlequino slows down his merry-go-round and widens it by opening both sticks, still pointing towards the interior. Make sure that the diabolos remain in contact with the string as long as possible.

For safety, add at least 30 cm to your string length.
In the merry-go-round with 3 diabolos, 2 are always together on the string.

When diabolo 3 is received, the other two are on the string and the fall of diabolo 3 will make diabolo 1 jump.

JUGGLING WITH FOUR DIABOLOS (and maybe more !) (fig. 94)

Throw 3 diabolos more than 4 meters high
(super giant merry-go-round) (see fig. 91, page 88).
An assistant can give you diabolo 4, in rotation, in the space between
diabolos 2 and 3.
The assistant is on your right and throws in
an oval trajectory.
Diabolo 4 takes off from your
assistant's string when diabolo 2 is
at its peak.

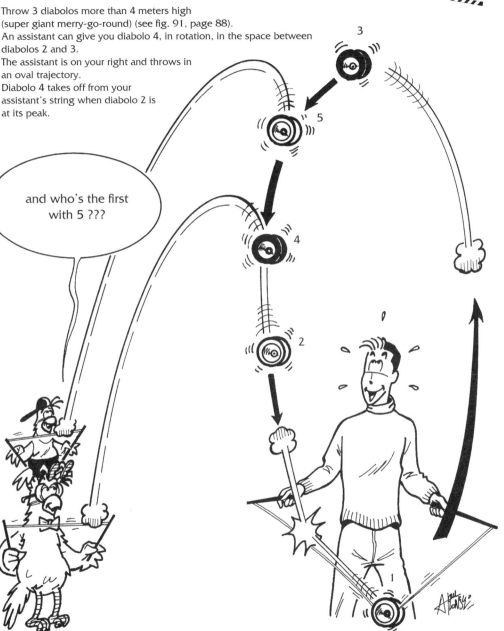

and who's the first
with 5 ???

ALREADY THEN !

(28 Juin 1908)

11me Fête Annuelle à Valabre de la Société des
" Excursionnistes Marseillais "
Concours de Diabolo

June 28th 1908 - Marseille - France - competition of diabolos ! Collection D. Schambacher - Geneva

DIABOLO VIRTUES !

De quoi parle-t-on à la ronde ?–
Que l'on vante à tous les échos,
Et qui fera le tour du monde ?–
— LE DIABOLO —

France 1907 - Collection D. Schambacher - Geneva

MISTER BABACHE : juggling for pleasure - a complete line of quality articles.

Bean bags
(18 kinds - multiple colour combinations)

Clubs
(for beginners, advanced and stage performers)

Swinging plates for all ages

Rings

Scarves to get
introduced to juggling

Devil sticks

Cigar boxes

Stage balls

Rebound balls

For over ten years at the service
of the juggling world
with articles and help
for all.
Quality - choice - advice -
experience - novelties.

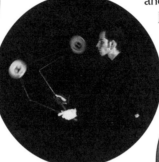

We would like to extend a very special THANK YOU to Thierry Nadalini, Jochen Schell and Jean Manuel Thoma, spectacular artists and great friends who have allowed us to demonstrate our methodology, the fantastic game of the diabolo and the healthy pleasure of juggling. They have collaborated wonderfully in our video programme « *DIABOLO FOLIES* ».

MISTER BABACHE DIABOLOS

A complete line of diabolos for everyone, for all tastes and skills.

SMALL DIABOLOS   : *discovery - games and gifts.*
- ARLEQUINO   magnificient multicoloured - rubber
- DIABOLINO   the toy - 4 plain colours - rubber
- BIRDIE   a super diabolo - 7 colours - rubber

MEDIUM DIABOLOS : *figures - first shows - schools.*
- STAR   the big toy - 9 brilliant colours
- MOON   phosphorescent for your night shows
- CRISTAL   transparent - 3 colours
- RUBBERKING   super PRO ! - 7 colours - rubber
- FLASHKING   the same in Rextan in 6 bright colours
- FLASHKING   the same in Rextan - colour GOLD or SILVER !

LARGE DIABOLOS   : *performance and stage - the Pros !*
- JUMBO   the favourite ! 6 colours - rubber
- ARLEQUIN   the most beautiful ! - 6 combinations of 2,3 or 4 colours
- EAGLE   the champion ! - 6 colours - rubber
- EAGLEFLASH   the same in Rextan in 6 bright colours

There is certainly a reliable and official distributor of **MISTER BABACHE** products in your region. They will help you to choose the best and most adapted diabolo for your technique and objectives. We will gladly send you the address of the distributor closest to your home.